SALADIN

Copyright © 2006 Marshall Editions

Conceived, edited and designed by Marshall Editions
The Old Brewery, 6 Blundell Street, London N7 9BH
www.quarto.com

First published in the UK in 2006 by
QED Publishing
A Quarto Group Company
226 City Road
London EC1V 2TT
www.qed-publishing.co.uk

A Catalogue record for this book is available from the British Library.

ISBN: 1 84538 336 2

Originated in Hong Kong by Modern Age
Printed and bound in China by Midas Printing Limited

For Marshall Editions:
Publisher: Richard Green
Commissioning editor: Claudia Martin
Art direction: Ivo Marloh
Editor: Johanna Geary
Picture manager: Veneta Bullen

Previous page: This impressive modern statue of Saladin was built outside the citadel in Damascus.
Opposite: Muslim cavalry (left) and Christian Crusaders (right) clash in the Holy Land during
the Crusades.

SALADIN

"EUROPEAN MERCHANTS SUPPLY
THE BEST WEAPONRY, CONTRIBUTING
TO THEIR OWN DEFEAT."

FIONA MACDONALD

CONTENTS

A MUSLIM YOUTH

1

STUDENT AND SOLDIER

2

CONQUERING AN EMPIRE

3

HERO OF THE CRUSADES

4

A MUSLIM YOUTH

وَكَادَ يُزَعْزِعُ الجِمَالَ السَّيرُ وَالنَّشَدُ

مَا الحَجُّ سَيرُكَ تَأوِيبًا وَادّلَاجَا وَلَا اعْتِمَالُكَ أَجْمَالًا وَأَحْدَاجَا

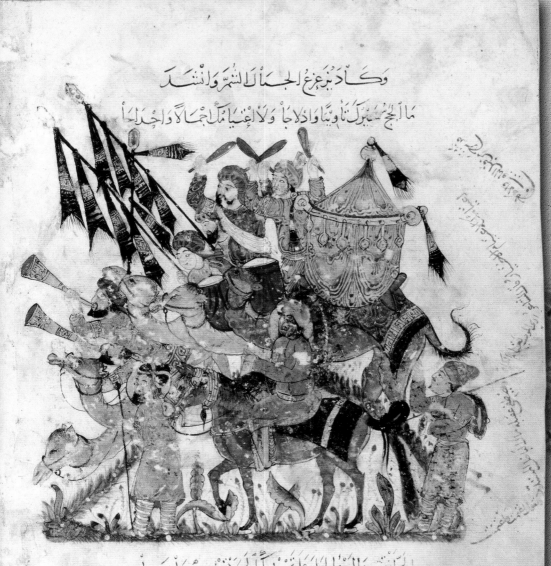

الحَجُّ أَن تَقصِدَ البَيتَ الحَرَامَ عَلَى نَحجٍ يَدُلُّ عَلَى الحَجِّ لَا تَبغِي بِهِ حَاجَا

وَ سَعيُكَ أَن بِالإنصَافِ مُتَّخِذًا رَدعَ الهَوَى هَادِيًا وَالحَقَّ مِنهَاجَا

The Governor's Son

Late one summer night in 1138, the city of Tikrit, now in Iraq, was quiet and peaceful. Suddenly, angry voices rang out from the castle, where Shirkuh, brother of the castle governor, argued with the captain of the guard. Minutes later, the captain lay dead, stabbed by Shirkuh.

At the same time, elsewhere in the castle, a baby boy was born. The baby's father was the castle governor, Najm al-Din Ayyub. He blessed his son with the words used to welcome all Muslim babies: 'In the name of God, the Compassionate, the Merciful.' But he had no time to celebrate the birth. The captain's murder meant that Najm al-Din's whole family was in danger – including Adatte, his wife, and their baby. They must leave the castle immediately or be arrested and punished along with the murderer.

Right: Baghdad was the capital of a rich and splendid Muslim empire. The city's wealth came from taxes, trade and farming. Muslim engineers used clever technology, like this waterwheel, to help farmers bring water to their fields to grow more crops to sell.

Previous page: Musicians play drums and trumpets to encourage Muslim pilgrims as they make the journey to Mecca in Arabia, the holiest city in the Muslim world.

Due to the problem of dating events in Saladin's life, some dates are approximate. 'c.' is an abbreviation of 'circa', meaning 'about'. The Roman calendar is used for all dates.

1071

Muslim *caliphs* fear Christian invasion after Turks from Central Asia, named Seljuks, defeat the Christian Byzantines.

Right: Muslim sailors, traders and boat-builders were the first people to make use of monsoon winds that blow at regular times each year across the Indian Ocean. They designed cargo ships, called *dhows*, with large sails to catch the winds, and sleek, curved hulls to ride the waves.

Until the murder brought shame to his family, Najm al-Din had been well-respected. He was rich, clever and trustworthy. He had been born in the Caucasus Mountains, where his father was a tribal chief. As a young man, he had travelled to Baghdad and worked for the *caliph* there. The caliph was the overlord and spiritual leader of the surrounding Muslim states. Friends at the caliph's court had helped Najm al-Din to become governor of Tikrit castle, but now he had to flee.

Najm al-Din chose a name for his new baby: Yusuf. Following tradition, he added 'Ibn Ayyub ibn Shadi', or 'son of Ayyub, grandson of Shadi'. Yusuf meant 'trouble and suffering', so it must have seemed suitable. Later, Yusuf ibn Ayyub won a glorious new name for himself as a Muslim leader. He became known as Al-Malik An-Nasir Salah al-Din, which means 'Mighty Defender, Righteousness of the Faith'. Europeans called him Saladin.

Saladin's birthday

Muslims use their own calendar. It begins in the year A.D. 622, when the first Muslim community was founded. Saladin was born in 532 of the Islamic calendar. This correlates to the period between September 1137 and September 1138 in the Roman calendar that we use today.

1096–1099

The First Crusade. Christian armies from Europe invade the Holy Land.

15 July 1099

Crusaders capture the city of Jerusalem from the Muslims and take control of the Holy Land.

Big City Life

Saladin's father decided to take his family to a place where the caliph's soldiers had no power to arrest them. He chose the city of Mosul, now in northern Iraq. It was ruled by Imad al-Din Zangi, a Seljuk Turkish ruler, who had taken it from the caliph in 1127. A number of Seljuk Turkish nobles, who were originally from Central Asia, had control over much of the Baghdad caliph's lands. Saladin's father and his brother Shirkuh both joined Zangi's army, as senior officers.

Mosul was a very ancient city. People had lived there for almost 8,000 years. In Saladin's day, it was a great trading centre. It lay close to the Silk Road, a network of desert tracks and mountain pathways that ran from China in the east to the Black Sea in the west. Merchants travelled along this route, carrying silk from China, gemstones from India and spices from the Southeast Asian islands.

Left: In Saladin's time, the city of Mosul was guarded by massive brick walls and gates that had survived since around 600 B.C. The gates were locked at sunset each evening to keep strangers out.

June 1138
Saladin is born in Tikrit.

1138
Saladin's family arrives in the city of Mosul, which is now in Iraq.

Muslin

Cloth-makers in Mosul wove a beautiful, smooth cotton fabric that was worn by rich and fashionable Europeans in Saladin's time. Mosul cloth became known as 'muslin'. It still has the same name today.

At Mosul, Silk Road merchants stopped for food and water and to sell their wares in its covered markets, or *souks*. They bargained with other traders selling perfumes from Arabia, ivory from Africa and pearls from the Persian Gulf. They also bought treasures made by Mosul's own craftsmen, who were famous for delicate glassware and metal dishes and bowls. Saladin would have seen all these goods, together with grain and vegetables from the surrounding countryside.

Mosul was home to many different peoples, mostly from Muslim lands. Saladin's family were Kurds, a proud Muslim people who had their own language, culture and traditions. Kurdish communities could be found in many parts of the Middle East. Kurds mostly lived as farmers, raising sheep and goats on mountain pastures. Kurdish people were famous for their music, poetry, dancing, horse-riding and for their fighting skills. Like Saladin's father, many Kurdish men worked for the Seljuk Turkish rulers or served in their armies as fierce *peshmergas*, or 'warriors who are not afraid to face death'.

Right: At Mosul and other Muslim cities, disputes between traders were heard by judges named *qadis*. Here, a qadi, seated on the right, settles a quarrel between buyers and sellers.

1138

Zangi captures the city of Homs in Syria. It controls routes linking the Silk Road with the Mediterranean Sea.

1139

Zangi besieges the rich city of Damascus, the capital of Syria.

Early Years at Home

Saladin and his family lived in Mosul for six or seven years. His father was often away from home, helping to organize Zangi's battle campaigns. These were troubled times in the Middle East. The Baghdad caliph had many enemies. They included Seljuk rulers, like Zangi; the Fatimids, who were rival Muslim rulers from Egypt; the Byzantines, who were the Christian emperors from Constantinople; and Crusaders. The Crusaders were Christian armies from Western Europe who had taken the Holy Land (the region around Jerusalem) from Muslim control by force.

Above: Wealthy Muslim homes, like Saladin's, were furnished with items from different parts of the Muslim world. This prayer mat was made in Turkey between A.D. 1000 and 1100.

Saladin was too young to understand these wars. Like other wealthy Muslim children of the period, he spent most of his time in the harem – the private women's rooms of a Muslim house. There, he was cared for by his mother and the female servants. They encouraged him to be respectful, truthful and obedient. They also taught him to worship God as a Muslim.

c. 1140
Young Saladin first begins to learn about the Muslim faith.

c. 1140
Zangi is the first Muslim ruler to declare *jihad*, meaning struggle or holy war, against the Christian Crusaders.

As a male child, Saladin would have been specially valued. The Muslim holy book, the Qur'an, taught Muslims that all children were gifts from God. They should be valued equally as 'the ornaments of this world'. But most Muslim families believed that boys were more important than girls, because sons could earn money to care for their parents when they were old and could not work any longer.

When they grew up, most Muslim boys also had greater opportunities than girls to be active in public life. Although Kurdish countrywomen worked outdoors on farms, the majority of Muslim women in cities like Mosul stayed at home except to attend religious services, celebrate religious festivals or visit relatives and close female friends.

Even so, wealthy Muslim women like Saladin's mother had many important responsibilities. They managed large households, cared for their husbands, raised their children, ordered food and furnishings, and supervised the servants and slaves around the home. If they chose, they could study or run their own businesses from home, as well. Poor women also worked hard in their homes, cooking, cleaning and caring for their families.

The Five 'Pillars' of Islam

Muslims believe that the following five actions are the 'pillars', or most important parts, of their faith:

• Worship Allah, 'The One God', and honour the Prophet Muhammad.
• Pray five times a day.
• Fast (go without food) during the holy month of *Ramadan*.
• Give to charity.
• Go on a pilgrimage, or *haj*, to the holy city of Mecca in Arabia.

c. 1140
Saladin's father and Uncle Shirkuh spend time away from home fighting in Zangi's army.

1140
Christian Crusaders in Jerusalem join with Muslims in Damascus to fight against Zangi.

Going to School

Saladin may have started to learn to read while he was still in the harem. Many wealthy Muslim women could read and write, and believed that a good education would give their children the best start in life. But it was more likely that Saladin began formal lessons when he was about seven years old. Then, he either went to school, or learned from a tutor at home.

Muslim schools were usually in mosques. These were beautiful buildings where devout Muslim men went to pray every day. Other Muslims went to their local mosque each Friday, the Muslim holy day, to listen to a preacher and to pray.

Saladin's early lessons were almost certainly based on the Qur'an. Like other pupils, Saladin had the challenging task of memorizing the whole text of the Qur'an, and reciting as much as possible.

Above: This precious copy of the Qur'an was handwritten, probably in Iraq, some time between A.D. 800 and 900. The Muslim artist used a style of calligraphy known as *Kufic* script, which features bold, geometric shapes.

1142

Byzantine emperor John II tries to establish control over the Crusaders in the Holy Land, but he fails.

1143

Manuel I becomes Byzantine emperor. He admires European culture and neglects his Middle Eastern lands.

Right: Pupils seated on the floor listen while two school-masters discuss a topic. Each pupil holds his own copy of the Qur'an, the basis of all lessons at a Muslim primary school.

It took two years for a pupil to learn the entire text of the Qur'an by heart, and most pupils never achieved this completely. Instead, they could only remember a few of their favourite passages, such as those quoted by preachers in the mosque or repeated in prayers.

The Qur'an is written in the Arabic language, so Muslim pupils learned to speak Arabic as well as their native language, as they chanted and memorized words from the holy book. Some also learned to read Arabic and to write it in a beautiful, flowing script that ran from right to left across the page. Sharing a single language helped to link Muslims all around the world. It allowed messages to travel over hundreds of miles without the need for translation. It also meant that Muslim scholars could pass on important new discoveries, and allowed Muslim rulers to make new plans involving people from lots of different regions.

Further education

Saladin was a clever boy who enjoyed studying. After learning from the Qur'an, he looked forward to attending a college, called a *madresseh*. There, senior pupils could study poetry, law, religion or practical sciences, such as medicine, engineering and astronomy. Muslim scholars were world leaders in all these areas.

1143
The Crusader king of Jerusalem, Fulk of Anjou, dies.

c. 1144
Saladin starts to study the Qur'an.

Muslim Civilization

The Muslim faith began in Arabia around A.D. 622. From there, it spread quickly – by the time Saladin was born in 1138, Muslim lands stretched from southern Spain and North Africa to China and India. These lands were home to a rich, multicultural civilization, which blended local traditions with new ideas from distant Muslim lands. Muslim scholars also carefully preserved discoveries made by past civilizations, especially the ancient Greeks and Egyptians, and used these to improve their own skills in science, medicine, astronomy and maths.

London

CHRISTIAN KINGDOMS

Paris

EUROPE

Cordoba · Mediterranean Sea

Tangier

TUNISIA

ALMORAVIDS AND ALMOHADS

A F R I C A

Timbuktu

Djenne

ATLANTIC OCEAN

Above: A diagram of a water pump from a *Treatise on Mechanical Procedures*, written by Muslim engineer Al-Djazari in 1206. As well as bringing water to dry Middle Eastern lands, Muslim engineers also helped Muslim armies by designing guns, explosives and siege engines – huge machines used to attack defensive walls.

Above: A silver vase, inlaid with copper, shows the high quality of metalwork produced in many Muslim lands. It was made in Egypt circa 1300. Similar metal goods were made in Mosul when Saladin lived there.

KEY

- Centre of government by a caliph
- Under Muslim rule/influence
- Under the Baghdad caliph's authority around A.D. 1100

MUSLIM PEOPLES

- **Seljuk Turks** – Central Asian nobles who controlled the Middle East from A.D. 1055.
- **Ghaznavids** – Turkish warriors who controlled north India and Afghanistan A.D. 977–1040.
- **Zaidis** – Shia Muslims who ruled Yemen from the eighth century A.D.

- **Fatimids** – Shia Muslims who ruled eastern North Africa from Cairo, A.D. 910–1171.
- **Almoravids and Almohads** – Ruled western North Africa and southern Spain c.1055–c.1200.
- **Karakhanids** – Ruled Central Asia c. A.D. 900–1100.

Constantinople

Tiflis

TURKEY

KARAKHANIDS

Samarkand

S E L J U K

SYRIA Mosul

A S I A

LEBANON HOLY LAND

Kabul

Baghdad

T U R K S

IRAN

Jerusalem *IRAQ* Basra

Lahore

FATIMIDS

Cairo

Multan

Persian Gulf

A R A B I A

G H A Z N A V I D S

Red Sea

Medina

Mecca

Arabian Sea

ZAIDIS

Bay of Bengal

Mogadishu

Mombasa

INDIAN OCEAN

Mozambique

Left: This minaret is 52 metres (173 ft) high and was built from sun-dried mud bricks at the caliph's private city of Samarra, near Baghdad, circa A.D. 850. Its spiral design shows how Muslim architects used their knowledge of mathematics to create some amazing buildings in lands without stone.

Living as a Muslim

When Saladin first went to the mosque, he probably sat in the women's gallery with his mother and other young children, hidden from adult male worshippers behind a curtain or screen. But now, as a schoolboy, Saladin was growing up fast. It would not be long before he could sit with the men in the mosque, join in their prayers and work with them.

Already, Saladin knew how to wash himself before entering a mosque and how to behave quietly in its prayer hall. At home, he could say daily prayers, give thanks to God before meals, and welcome visitors with the Muslim greeting, '*As-salaam Alaykum*, Peace be with you'. He was still too young to fast during the holy month of Ramadan or give money to charity, but he knew these religious duties would soon be part of his life. There was one more step for Saladin to take before becoming a Muslim man. When he was about six, it was time to be circumcized. Muslims believed this custom helped men stay healthy. It also proved that a man was a member of a Muslim family or tribe.

Right: Inside the mosque at Basra, now in Iraq, glass lamps hang from arches surrounding the prayer hall. Male worshippers sit before the preacher. From the tower, or minaret, on top of the building, people are called to prayer.

c. 1144
Saladin starts to learn how to read Arabic.

c. 1144
Saladin is circumcized.

Left: Trumpeters and men carrying brightly coloured banners ride in a noisy procession through the streets of a Muslim town. Similar processions marked all kinds of important events, from circumcisions and success in memorizing the Qur'an, to victories in battle.

Like other important events, circumcision was celebrated by a splendid party, with lots of food, music and dancing. Sometimes men and boys also led joyful processions through the streets. Favourite party dishes included a whole sheep or goat that had been roasted over an open fire. This was served with a mound of rice, fruit, nuts and spices, called *pilaf*, as well as stuffed, baked vegetables; iced fruit syrup, called sherbet; and sweet, sticky pastries that were scented with rose water. There were also plenty of delicious fresh fruits such as apricots or melons.

Circumcized boys were soundly congratulated by everyone. They had now become real men! They were also given plenty of presents and new clothes. In a wealthy family such as Saladin's, gifts might include lots of sporting equipment, an ornate chess set, a trained hawk that was used to hunt small animals or even a new pony.

Saladin the sportsman

Throughout his life, Saladin loved horses, especially thoroughbreds (pure breeds) from Arabia. It was said that he could remember the pedigree (ancestry) of all the fine horses he had ever come across. Galloping through the desert, hunting deer and playing a kind of fast, furious hockey on horseback, called polo, were his favourite sports.

1144
Ibn Shabbad, the Muslim scholar and scribe who admired Saladin and wrote his biography, is born.

1144
The Seljuk leader Zangi leads his army toward the Crusader state of Edessa.

STUDENT AND
SOLDIER

Frontline Fortress

When Saladin was about seven years old, his world changed once again. Around 1144, his family left the multicultural city of Mosul, the only home that young Saladin could remember. They moved south, to Baalbek (now in Lebanon), because Zangi appointed Saladin's father to command the castle there. Life in a castle that stood at the foot of wild, rugged mountains was certainly going to be different.

Like Mosul, Baalbek had been conquered from the caliph by the Seljuk ruler Zangi. Now it was in a dangerous position on the frontline between the Seljuks and the Christian Crusaders. In 1128, Zangi had captured the city of Aleppo from Crusader control, and in 1144, his troops conquered the nearby state of Edessa from the Crusaders. Surely, the Crusaders would try to win both back.

Although it was dangerous to live there, the castle must have been an exciting place for a young boy like Saladin. Like other Muslim forts, Baalbek was built of stone.

Previous page: This pottery figure shows a Muslim warrior on horseback. He is wearing a pointed helmet and carrying a round shield and sharp sword.

Designed for defence

Baalbek castle's design included some of the best Muslim architectural features, such as narrow entrances and dark passageways which confused attackers trying to enter. By exploring the castle and talking to soldiers on guard duty, Saladin would have learned a lot about castle defences. This information proved useful in his later career.

1144
Zangi captures the Crusader state of Edessa. It is the first Crusader state to be taken back by Muslims.

1144
Saladin's family moves to Zangi's fortress at Baalbek.

It had massive walls and gates that were protected by huge lookout towers. The castle guarded the route for armies marching north.

Baalbek was strongly defended, but it relied on local people for supplies of food and wood. From the castle, Saladin could see nomad Arab families, called *Bedu*, who lived in tents in the desert and raised flocks of sheep and goats. He may also have met timber merchants from the valleys of Lebanon to the west, where magnificent cedar trees grew. He probably heard rumours about a mysterious brotherhood called the Assassins. They lived in remote mountain hideouts and were ready to kill to defend their unorthodox Muslim ideas.

Below: A detail from a Christian manuscript shows Muslim soldiers with bows and arrows defending their castle against Christian troops armed with swords.

1145
A new Great Mosque is built in Zangi's city, Mosul.

1145
The most important Muslim book about maths, *Algebra*, by al-Kwarizmi, is translated into English.

والبابُ السَّابِعُ مِنَ العَمَلِ بِالسَّيفِ وأسمُّهُ المُنَجِّمَ
وهوَانكَ اذا دَفَعتَ مِنَ المِنصَفِ وحَصَلَ السَّيفُ فِى شَمالِكَ وأنتَ دائِرٌ فِى الَّا ورد
قَدَرتَ عَلَى حالَكَ غَراصِرَ بِيَدِكَ اليُمنَى لِاقامِ السَّيفِ بِحِدِّدِ مَخَرِيدِهِ واصرِبهِ شَمالًا
مِنِ اذنِ الفَرَسِ اليُسرَى لِاكمَلِهِ الاسرِ واتَّحِ مِنِ كِملَهِ الاسرَ اليِ كِملَهِ الَّا بِمِنِ
شُمالِ السَّيفِ بِيَدِكَ اليِ قَدامِ جِهَنِكَ قَلِ مَيلِ السَّيفِ فَلَهُ حَولُ وجُهَكَ وانقَصِهِ

Left: A Muslim soldier gallops on a fine war horse in this Persian manuscript painted around 1371. The artist captured the sense of excitement that Saladin and his men felt when riding for sport or in war.

Almost certainly, Saladin started to learn how to fight while his family lived at Baalbek. All Middle Eastern men needed to know how to handle typical Muslim weapons – powerful bows and arrows, long spears and deadly sharp curved swords. Saladin also had to learn how to ride a horse in battle, by charging toward enemies, then suddenly swerving sideways and striking out at them as he rode by. He might have practised 'hit-and-run' attacks. This involved shooting arrows as he rode toward a target, then turning around in the saddle to keep on shooting as he galloped away to safety. This was a favourite tactic of Seljuk Turkish armies, and very successful against enemy forces who moved slowly on foot.

Saladin's father might have passed on his experience of planning battles, leading troops and organizing supplies of weapons, armour and food.

c. 1145
Saladin starts to learn how to fight.

1145
In Europe, the pope calls for a Second Crusade against Muslims in the Holy Land.

He probably also told Saladin about brutal sieges, when attacking troops surrounded enemy cities or castles until everyone trapped inside surrendered – or starved to death.

To help him ride and fight, Saladin probably changed the way he dressed around this time. In Mosul, where summer temperatures rise well over 40°C (100°F), most people wore long, cool robes. Away from the big cities, however, Kurdish and Turkish people chose to wear trousers. These were much more suitable for riding on horseback, or for running and fighting.

What did Saladin look like?

Like most Kurdish people, Saladin had olive-brown skin, black hair and brown eyes. As a child, he was smaller and thinner than other boys of the same age. Perhaps because of this, he was not very excited about fighting but preferred to read or study. As an adult, Saladin became tough, fit and strong, although he remained short and slender all his life.

Kurdish women covered their trousers with a knee-length robe, belted at the waist and trimmed with bands of embroidery. Often their robes had graceful pointed sleeves. Kurdish men wore shirts, waistcoats or jackets, and a wide sash around their waist. In wartime, they added a tunic of chain mail or a jerkin (sleeveless jacket) made of leather and plates of metal, plus a rounded metal helmet topped with a spike.

Kurdish tunics and trousers fulfilled Muslim religious rules: they did not reveal the body or draw attention to the wearer. Kurdish women did not veil their faces, but usually covered their hair with embroidered caps or scarves. Kurdish men wore skullcaps and turbans, or sheepskin hats for warmth.

1146
Zangi is murdered after a drunken quarrel.

1146
Zangi's son, Nur al-Din (born 1118), takes over his father's army and lands.

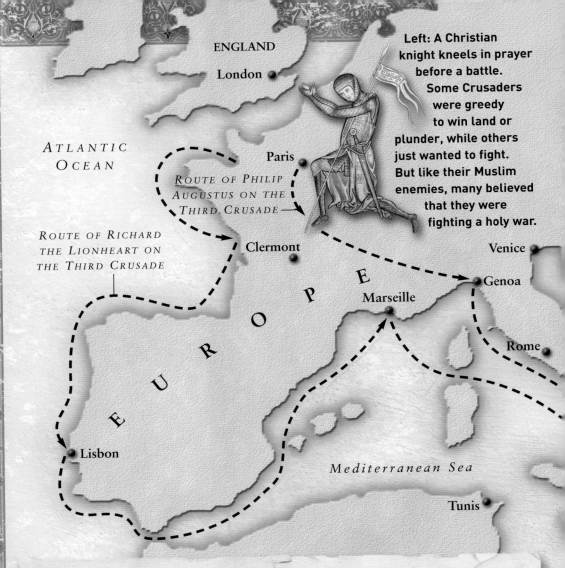

ENGLAND

London

ATLANTIC
OCEAN

Paris

*ROUTE OF PHILIP
AUGUSTUS ON THE
THIRD CRUSADE* →

*ROUTE OF RICHARD
THE LIONHEART ON
THE THIRD CRUSADE*

Clermont

Venice

Genoa

E U R O P E

Marseille

Rome

Lisbon

Mediterranean Sea

Tunis

Left: A Christian
knight kneels in prayer
before a battle.
Some Crusaders
were greedy
to win land or
plunder, while others
just wanted to fight.
But like their Muslim
enemies, many believed
that they were
fighting a holy war.

The Middle East in Saladin's Time

For many centuries, the Middle East had been Muslim territory. However, by Saladin's time, many of the Middle Eastern lands were occupied by foreign powers and divided. Since 1099, Crusaders from Europe had set up Christian states along the eastern coast of the Mediterranean Sea. Christian Byzantine emperors based in Constantinople also threatened to attack the Muslim territories. Middle Eastern lands that were still held by Muslims were divided among rival rulers who fought among themselves. The caliphs, who ruled from Baghdad, were no longer able to keep control over all the states. The rival rulers in the region included Fatimids, Seljuks and Zaidis. Army commanders like Zangi and Nur al-Din realized the grave danger that the Muslim states were in. Until Muslim rulers could stop quarrelling and Muslim lands could be re-united, they remained a target for the Christian Crusaders.

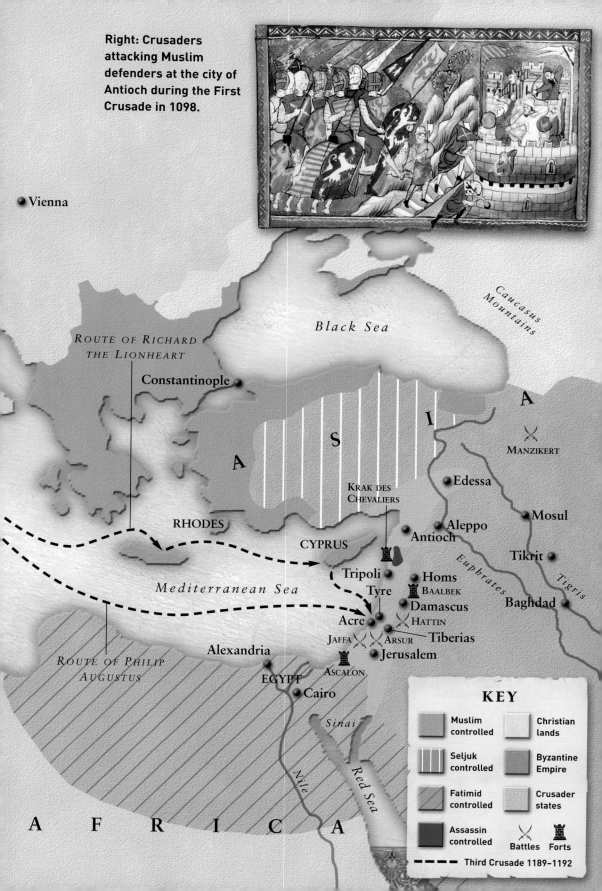

Right: Crusaders attacking Muslim defenders at the city of Antioch during the First Crusade in 1098.

Vienna

Caucasus Mountains

Black Sea

ROUTE OF RICHARD THE LIONHEART

Constantinople

A   S   I   A

MANZIKERT

Edessa

KRAK DES CHEVALIERS

Mosul

RHODES

Aleppo

Antioch

CYPRUS

Euphrates

Tripoli

Homs

Tikrit

Tigris

Tyre

BAALBEK

Baghdad

Mediterranean Sea

Damascus

Acre

HATTIN

Alexandria

JAFFA   ARSUR   Tiberias

ROUTE OF PHILIP AUGUSTUS

Jerusalem

EGYPT

ASCALON

Cairo

Sinai

Nile

Red Sea

A F R I C A

KEY

Muslim controlled	Christian lands
Seljuk controlled	Byzantine Empire
Fatimid controlled	Crusader states
Assassin controlled	⚔ Battles 🏰 Forts

– – – Third Crusade 1189–1192

Extra Duties

Unlike young people today, Saladin had little free time to play and relax. Everywhere in the medieval world, children were expected to make themselves useful. When he was not studying or learning how to fight, Saladin had to help other members of his family with chores and tasks. This might involve welcoming friends when his father was away, escorting his mother when she left the castle, or keeping a watchful eye on his young brothers and sisters.

Above: Two Seljuk Turkish warriors, pictured on a pottery drinking bowl made in Syria around 1200. Saladin would have lived alongside fighting men like these when he started to work for his uncle Shirkuh.

When Saladin was aged 14, his father decided that he should start work full-time. So, in 1152, he sent Saladin away from Baalbek Castle to help Shirkuh, Saladin's uncle. In spite of his murderous past, Shirkuh had won fame fighting for the Seljuk Turkish noble, Zangi. But now Zangi was dead, and Shirkuh had joined the army led by Zangi's son, the commander Nur al-Din.

1147
Armies of the Second Crusade are defeated by Seljuk Turks at the Battle of Dorylaeum near Constantinople.

1148
The surviving Christian soldiers of the Second Crusade arrive in the Holy Land.

Nur al-Din was already ruler of the city of Aleppo in Syria, but he had great ambitions. He wanted to rule all of Syria and conquer the other Muslim lands that lay nearby. He also hoped to drive the Christian Crusader forces out of the Middle East for good.

Away from his father's control, young Saladin had a lot more freedom than he had ever had before. His duties kept him busy, but he may have enjoyed at least some of them. Saladin probably had to help look after Shirkuh's horses, clean his weapons and armour, run messages and write letters for him. Possibly, he also served food and drink to Shirkuh and his fellow warriors when they relaxed after a hard day's work. Because Saladin had studied so much, they may have asked him to recite some poems in elegant Arabic. In turn, he may have listened to them singing noisy Kurdish warrior songs.

Nur al-Din

The famous army commander Nur al-Din won several important battles. As well as being a great military leader, he was also known as a fair and honest ruler, and for his devotion to the Muslim faith. He lived very simply, giving most of the money from his conquests to mosques, hospitals and schools. This led his wife to complain that she never had any nice clothes to wear.

Although Shirkuh and the other soldiers were forbidden to consume alcohol by Muslim religious laws, they seem to have enjoyed drinking wine – and to have given some to young Saladin as well. These teenage years are the only time when Saladin is said to have shown bad behaviour. People said he preferred wine, sports and girlfriends to religion.

When his father and Nur al-Din went on a pilgrimage to the holy city of Mecca in Arabia, the young Saladin did not accompany them.

1152

Saladin goes to work for his uncle Shirkuh, who is an officer in Nur al-Din's army.

1153

Crusaders build a new Church of the Holy Sepulchre in Jerusalem.

A New Home

As well as finding him a job, Saladin's father decided that it was time for his son to get married. Perhaps he hoped marriage might tame his son's wild behaviour and encourage him to settle into a quieter way of life. Following tradition, Saladin's parents chose his bride. This was the usual custom in most medieval Muslim families. Kurdish women like Saladin's mother were famous for their matchmaking skills.

We know very little about Saladin's wife. Saladin's parents made sure that she came from a good Muslim family. She was probably around the same age as Saladin, about 14 or 15, when she wed. It seems likely that Saladin grew to be fond of her, since he did not divorce her, or swiftly choose to have extra wives – Muslim religious law allowed men to have four wives, as long as they treated them all equally. Medieval historians reported that Saladin and his wife had 16 or 17 children, though this may be an exaggeration to make Saladin seem extra-powerful.

In 1154, Nur al-Din won a brilliant victory. His armies took the historic city of Damascus from the caliph in Baghdad.

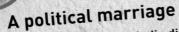

A political marriage

Later in his career, Saladin did take a second wife, but purely for political reasons. In 1176, he married the widow of his old commander, Nur al-Din. The marriage made Saladin step-father of Nur al-Din's young son and heir. This helped him claim the right to rule Nur al-Din's lands.

c. 1153
Saladin gets married when he is aged about 14 or 15.

1154
Nur al-Din captures Damascus and makes it his capital. Saladin goes to live there.

Above: Graceful domes, arches, and arcades at the Great Mosque in Damascus, Syria. The mosque was built around A.D. 700 on the site of an earlier Roman temple. Saladin almost certainly visited this mosque while he lived in Damascus.

This brought the whole of Syria under Nur al-Din's control. He moved his headquarters to Damascus, where he built a luxurious palace surrounded by shady gardens with fountains and pools. Along with Shirkuh, who was one of Nur al-Din's most trusted officers, Saladin went to live there.

Damascus soon became Saladin's favourite city. He continued to work for Shirkuh, learning more about fighting, government, politics and law. But he also had time to continue his religious studies. Damascus had famous mosques and wonderful colleges and libraries. There were also Muslim mystics, called *Sufis*, who taught their followers to seek God through meditation and to develop inner feelings of calm, self-control, tolerance, patience and understanding. Saladin later became famous for all of these qualities.

1157
Prince Richard Plantagenet is born in England. He becomes Richard I, Saladin's greatest Christian enemy.

1163
The Crusader King of Jerusalem starts to attack Muslim lands in Egypt.

CONQUERING AN
EMPIRE

... ... guerroit q
... ... quil auoient p̄ leur eloie
haut home eloient de matin ap̄

R uous appareille
que con bien mor
nierent que sil ...

Rival Rulers

At times, Saladin's uncle Shirkuh must have worried about his nephew. Although he was now an adult with family responsibilities, Saladin still loved studying. He spent all his free time – when he was not playing polo – at madressehs in Damascus, listening to scholars and debating with other students. Was this really what a man from a Kurdish fighting family should do? Surely it was time for Saladin to prove his bravery on the battlefield. There were enemies all around!

The Christian Crusader states often fought with their Muslim neighbours. When Saladin was a young man, Crusaders controlled three Christian-ruled states in the Middle East (Edessa, Tripoli and Antioch), as well as the holy city of Jerusalem. Muslims fought one another as well as with Crusaders. The caliph in Baghdad and the Fatimid family who ruled Egypt were great rivals.

Previous page: In this Christian medieval manuscript, Crusader knights wearing helmets (right) charge against Muslim troops (left).

Right: Fatimid troops ride out from a well-defended city in Egypt to fight against the Crusaders. The Fatimid soldiers on the city watchtowers are armed with typical Muslim bows and arrows.

1163
The new, energetic Crusader king, Amalric, is crowned in Jerusalem.

1163
Amalric leads a Crusader army to attack the Fatimid rulers of Egypt.

Their quarrels were especially fierce because they belonged to different branches of the Muslim religion – the caliph in Baghdad was a Sunni Muslim, while the Fatimid rulers in Egypt were Shia Muslims.

Since 1055, there had been a third powerful Muslim force in the Middle East: the Seljuk Turks. Seljuk rulers, like Zangi and his son, Nur al-Din, controlled a large part of the caliph's land.

Now, in 1163, Fatimids, Seljuks and Crusaders were all fighting against each other. The Seljuks wanted to overthrow the Fatimids and seize their treasures, which included a glowing red ruby half the size of a man's hand. They also had a bigger, bolder ambition: to unite Egypt and the Middle East into one powerful Islamic state.

Religious differences

Saladin and his family belonged to the Sunni branch of the Muslim religion, as did the Seljuk nobles and most people that they ruled. The caliph in Baghdad was the leader of the Sunni community. Sunni Muslims follow the *Sunna*, or example, set by the Prophet Muhammad. They are also guided by *Hadith*, the holy sayings collected by Muslim scholars.

The Fatimid rulers of Egypt belonged to the Shia branch of the Muslim faith. There were small Shia communities in many Middle Eastern lands. Shia Muslims are guided by *Imams* (holy leaders), descended from Ali, the Prophet Muhammad's son-in-law.

The Crusaders wanted Egypt as a base for defending the Holy Land. It had good harbours and fresh water. Like the Seljuks, they also dreamed of a united Middle East – under Christian rule.

In September 1163, when Saladin was aged 25, the Crusaders invaded Egypt. The Fatimids and the Seljuks set aside their differences to fight their common enemy. Shirkuh, with Saladin as his second-in-command, led Nur al-Din's Seljuk soldiers and forced the Crusaders back to Jerusalem.

1163
Shirkuh and Saladin defend the Fatimids in Egypt from the Crusaders.

1163
The Seljuk ruler Nur al-Din calls for jihad by all Muslims against the Christian Crusaders.

Taking Control

In 1164, Crusaders from Jerusalem attacked Egypt for a second time. Again, Shirkuh and Saladin were able to help drive them away. But in 1167, the Crusaders were joined by fresh soldiers, who had travelled by sea from Europe and landed in Egypt. Now the Fatimids were in real danger!

Shirkuh led Nur al-Din's best troops to fight these new invaders, trusting Saladin to defend the rest of Egypt. Bravely, Saladin and his men stopped a force of Crusaders from breaking through the walls of Alexandria, Egypt's second largest city. The Crusader army besieged Alexandria for a whole month. Throughout this time, Saladin, his troops and the city's inhabitants were without fresh weapons, food or water, but they did not surrender. At last, Shirkuh returned with his soldiers and drove the attacking Crusaders away. Later reports praised Saladin for treating his Christian enemies with fairness and mercy during the siege of Alexandria.

Below: This portrait from an Egyptian manuscript shows Saladin in the robe and turban of a Sultan of Egypt. He took total control of Egypt in 1171, when he was 33 years old.

1164
A massive earthquake hits Syria. Both Muslims and Crusaders are killed.

1167
Saladin shows courage and mercy while defending the city of Alexandria.

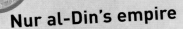

Nur al-Din's empire

Thanks to Shirkuh and Saladin, by 1169 the Seljuk ruler Nur al-Din controlled a vast empire that stretched from Iraq to Egypt. It united Sunni and Shia Muslims in one single state under Sunni rule. This ended political divisions between Muslim governments that had lasted for hundreds of years – though different groups of Muslims still quarrelled over religious beliefs.

Late in 1167, the Fatimids made a peace treaty with the Crusaders, paying them four million gold coins to stop attacking Egypt. To many Sunni Muslims, including Nur al-Din, Shirkuh and Saladin, this agreement seemed deeply shameful. It only strengthened their long-held suspicion of the Fatimids.

The peace treaty did not last long, however. In 1168, Crusader armies marched on Egypt for the fourth time. The Fatimids appealed for help to be sent immediately. In 1169, Nur al-Din's troops, led by Shirkuh and Saladin, defeated the Crusaders. But instead of returning home to Damascus, both Saladin and Shirkuh stayed in Egypt, deciding to take control of the country from the Fatimids.

Shirkuh declared himself to be the chief minister, or *vizir*, of Egypt, with Saladin as his helper. Both took their orders directly from Nur al-Din, even though they pretended to be 'helping' the Fatimids rule.

Winning control of Egypt was the peak of Shirkuh's brave but brutal career. Within just a few months, he was dead – probably from overeating. Quickly, Saladin seized Shirkuh's position as chief minister. He vowed loyalty to Nur al-Din and to his spiritual lord, the caliph in Baghdad.

Just two years later, most mysteriously, the last Fatimid ruler of Egypt collapsed and died. Many people suspected that Saladin had poisoned him.

1169
Shirkuh takes control of Egypt, to 'help' the Fatimids rule. He soon dies, and Saladin replaces him.

1171
The last Fatimid ruler dies, leaving Saladin in total control of Egypt.

Fatimid Egypt

From 1171, Saladin became ruler of Egypt. Although he had overlords – Nur al-Din and the caliph of Baghdad – he was in control of the country from day to day. Egypt was home to a splendid civilization. Its people had inherited knowledge and skills in building, engineering, mathematics, science and astronomy from their ancestors, the ancient Egyptians. They had also learned from the ancient Greeks and Romans, who, like Saladin, had conquered and ruled the country. Egypt had good farmland, fresh water, fine cities and magnificent monuments. Scholars from many lands came to study at its schools and libraries. Egypt had been Muslim since A.D. 639, but it also remained home to Jewish and Christian families. The Fatimid dynasty came to power in A.D. 969. They added to Egypt's riches by building a new capital city, Cairo, with many fine buildings and works of art, and by conquering land in Sinai and North Africa.

Above: This mosque, built by Ibn Tulun, Turkish governor of Fustat (now Cairo), circa A.D. 868, was one of the most famous Muslim buildings in Egypt. Saladin may have walked in this courtyard. Muslims met here before entering the main hall of the mosque to say prayers.

Right: Egyptian metalworkers were admired throughout the Muslim world. This bronze statue, perhaps used as an incense-burner, was made around A.D. 1050 in the shape of a magical monster called a griffin.

Below: This amazing jug was carved from a single chunk of rock crystal circa A.D. 950. It may have been used by the Fatimid rulers in Egypt, or sent by them as a gift to other powerful people to impress them with the wealth of Egypt and the skill of Egyptian craftsmen.

Above: Since ancient Egyptian times, engineers built Nilometers to measure the rise and fall of water flowing along the River Nile. Farming in Egypt depended on the regular yearly arrival of Nile flood-waters, and their disappearance three to four months later.

Right: Fatimid rulers in Egypt collected taxes from merchants and traders to pay for fine buildings and soldiers' wages. These Egyptian traders are weighing heavy bundles of goods.

Fresh Conquests

Saladin's rule in Egypt started well, but, by May 1174, things were going badly for Muslims elsewhere in the Middle East. A fleet of ships crowded with Crusaders headed for the Holy Land. In Iran and Iraq, Shia Muslims felt bitter about the end of Fatimid power. Worst of all, Nur al-Din had just died. Who could possibly replace him as a warrior or a ruler? Who could calm, unite and defend all the Muslim lands?

Saladin believed he was the right man for that task. He would lead the Muslims! For almost 20 years, he had served in Nur al-Din's army. He had watched, listened and learned as Nur al-Din and Shirkuh made battle plans. In the past few years in Egypt, Saladin had proved that he could fight, lead men and run a government. Now a new duty called him. Like Nur al-Din, he must unite Muslim lands and save them from the Christian Crusaders.

How could this be done? Saladin thought he knew. He hurried north to Damascus and announced that he would be the next king of Syria – not Nur al-Din's 11-year-old son and heir, Malik al-Salih Ismail. Nur al-Din's old comrades were horrified at Saladin's actions. 'This is treason!' they cried.

A generous man

Even while he was fighting, Saladin won praise for his kindness and generosity. Muslim writers told how Nur al-Din's youngest daughter was brought to see Saladin soon after he had captured a fine castle from her brother, Malik al-Salih Ismail. Saladin asked her what she would like as a present. She asked for the castle to be given back to her brother – and Saladin agreed.

1174

Saladin and Nur al-Din quarrel. Nur al-Din wants to fight the Crusaders. Saladin wants to unite Muslim lands first.

1174

Nur al-Din dies. Legally, his young son should inherit his power.

They wanted Malik al-Salih Ismail to be king, not a power-hungry scholar from a barbaric Kurdish tribe. Nur al-Din's old comrades, known as the Zangids, declared war on Saladin. But Saladin had brought an army to protect him. He seized Damascus, married Nur al-Din's widow, and set out to win the rest of Nur al-Din's lands.

As he fought, Saladin soon found that he had other Muslim enemies. Rival Seljuk army officers envied his sudden rise to power. City governors, especially in Syria and Iraq, said that Saladin had betrayed his old lord, Nur al-Din. Saladin, however, believed that he was right, and battled on – against both Zangids and Crusaders.

Below: Soldiers in Saladin's army, riding into battle on horseback. They are carrying round or heart-shaped shields decorated with crests. Their horses wear long surcoats, which are like fitted cloaks. Surcoats may have helped protect the horses from biting flies in the desert.

1174
Saladin goes to Damascus and names himself king. He proclaims the start of a new dynasty: the Ayyubids.

1174
War starts between Saladin and Nur al-Din's son and his supporters. It lasts for 12 years.

The Assassins

Saladin faced another, mysterious enemy – a secret brotherhood called the Assassins. Some people believed that the Assassins were wizards who could fly. Others thought they were ghosts or devils. Everyone agreed that the Assassins were ruthless killers who murdered powerful people who did not share their religious opinions.

In reality the Assassins were a small group of Shia Muslims with unusual views. Between 1174 and 1176, they tried to kill Saladin several times. For protection, Saladin kept bodyguards on duty day and night to stop strangers from approaching. He wore thick leather armour and kept his sword always by his side. Even so, in 1175, the Assassins nearly killed him – twice. His cheek was slashed by an Assassin's knife, and he was stabbed in the chest.

Below: The Valley of the Assassins in Iran. The Assassins built hideouts in hostile territory like this to make it very difficult for an attacking army to survive.

1176

Saladin threatens the Assassins, then makes a peace deal with them.

1183

Saladin conquers Aleppo, the most important city in northern Syria.

Left: The strong castle at Aleppo, which Saladin took from Zangid forces in 1183.'

Saladin decided to confront his Assassin attackers. In 1176, he marched his army to the Assassins' headquarters in the mountains. Then he issued a stern warning. Unless the Assassins stopped trying to kill him, he would flatten their castles. The Assassins remained defiant, but, surprisingly, Saladin did not fight. Instead, he went home quietly. People said Saladin had made a secret peace deal with the Assassins.

After 1176, the Assassins made fewer attacks on Saladin, but his life was still in danger from them. If Saladin left home, he slept in a wooden tower instead of a tent like other army commanders. It was the only way to stay safe.

Making peace with the Assassins left Saladin free to continue his fight to rule Nur al-Din's empire. It took 12 years of battles, sieges and diplomacy until at last, in 1186, he succeeded. But still Saladin could not rest. Now that he had united Muslim lands, his duty was to turn all his might against the Crusaders!

War of words

Once, Saladin sent a letter warning the Assassins to stop attacking him. The Assassin leader wrote back to say what he thought of Saladin: 'We have read your letter... and, by God, it is astonishing to find a fly buzzing in an elephant's ear... Others before you have also threatened us, and we destroyed them...'

1186

Saladin conquers his old home town of Mosul, which is now in Iraq.

1186

Saladin controls Nur al-Din's empire. All the Muslim lands in the Middle East are united.

HERO OF THE
CRUSADES

Holy War

In March 1187, a group of Muslim merchants and pilgrims stumbled along a mountain pathway. Their journey from Cairo to Damascus was long, and their route ran through land where Crusaders and Saladin's armies were at war. Both armies had agreed to a truce in the fighting, so the travellers felt safe enough to leave home. But as they entered a valley, they were attacked and killed by a band of Crusader knights.

Merciful conqueror

Saladin could be ruthless. He killed 300 top Crusader knights after the Battle of Hattin, executing their leader, Reynald of Chatillon, with his own sword. But because Jerusalem surrendered, he treated Christians there more mercifully. He let old or sick people go free, together with anyone else who could pay a ransom. He sold the rest of the Christians as slaves.

Previous page: Saladin's soldiers, on horseback, lead Christian prisoners away from a ruined, burning city in a picture painted by a Christian artist circa 1255.

When Saladin heard of this ambush, he decided he must act. He besieged the greatest Crusader castle, Krak des Chevaliers. He also sent his son, al-Adfal, to raid the Crusaders' lands. By June 1187, Saladin had assembled a huge army of more than 20,000 men.

Saladin's plan was simple – he would set a trap. He sent his soldiers to attack a Christian city, Tiberias, hoping the Crusaders would hurry to defend it. To do this, the Crusaders would have to cross a desert in the scorching sun. As Saladin hoped, the Crusaders set out. But they found that there was no water – and nowhere to hide.

March 1187
The Crusader knight Reynald of Chatillon attacks a group of Muslim pilgrims and traders.

April–May 1187
Saladin besieges the Crusader castle Krak des Chevaliers in Syria. His son raids Christian lands.

Saladin's men shot them with arrows and choked them with black smoke made by burning desert plants. Finally, they surrounded the Crusaders on a mountain called the Horns of Hattin. Thousands of Crusaders died, and Saladin made the rest his prisoners.

Above: Muslim and Christian cavalry clash during the Battle of Hattin in this illustration from a European medieval manuscript.

Saladin then led his army into Crusader lands. In October 1187, he surrounded Jerusalem. For a week, his army fired arrows over the gates and used giant catapults, called mangonels, to batter the city walls. The Christians inside had to surrender.

It was a glorious victory! After almost 100 years, the holy city belonged to Muslims once again. One Muslim writer recorded: 'People raised their voices in praise of God... Eyes were filled with tears of joy.' Saladin sat 'most humbly and graciously... with his face gleaming with happiness'.

4 July 1187
Saladin defeats the Crusaders at the Battle of Hattin.

July 1187
An advance guard of Crusaders arrives at the city of Tyre.

Crusaders from Europe

Above: This medieval map, made by Christian scholars, shows the city of Jerusalem at the centre of the world. Jerusalem was holy to people from three great faiths: Muslims, Christians and Jews.

The capture of Jerusalem made Saladin a hero to Muslims. The pope, Urban III, collapsed and died when he heard the news. But Saladin could not rest and celebrate his victory. He was determined to fight on and defeat the Crusader kingdoms. By the end of the next year, 1188, Saladin had captured 50 Crusader castles – and almost all the Holy Land.

After nearly two years of battles, marches and sieges, Saladin's soldiers were tired. They wanted to go home and see their families. Saladin gave them time off to rest and recover from their injuries, but he would not let them leave. He still needed them to fight.

Saladin's spies told him that a new army of Crusaders was getting ready to leave Europe. They had vowed to defeat Saladin and recapture Jerusalem. Already, an advance guard had landed close to Tyre in Lebanon. Their arrival had stopped Saladin from capturing Tyre late in 1187. It was his first failure in battle against Christians and it meant that the Crusaders still had a base in the Holy Land where they could shelter soldiers and receive fresh supplies.

Within three years, shiploads of Christian soldiers were arriving in the Holy Land from Italy. They were led by Europe's three greatest rulers.

October 1187
Saladin recaptures Jerusalem from the Crusaders.

October 1187
Pope Urban III dies after hearing that Saladin has captured Jerusalem. The next pope calls for a new crusade.

> *'Jihad [holy war] had taken a mighty hold on his heart and all his being... he thought of nothing but the means to pursue it.'*
> **Description of Saladin by medieval Muslim writer Beha al-Din**

These were Richard I 'the Lionheart' of England, Philip II 'Augustus the Honourable' of France and Frederick Barbarossa from Germany. They had been recruiting armies, and by 1190, they were ready.

This Third Crusade had been specially blessed by the new pope, Gregory VIII. He promised that God would forgive the sins of each Christian soldier who fought in the Holy Land – so they need not fear punishment in Hell after they died. The pope added that, if Crusaders were killed fighting, it would be even better. They would be holy martyrs and they would be sure of a glorious place in Heaven.

Above: Christian Crusaders capturing Jerusalem from its Muslim rulers in 1099, during the First Crusade. Saladin vowed a jihad to win back the city for Muslims. In 1187, he succeeded.

1187–88
Saladin captures over 50 castles from the Crusaders.

1190
The armies of the Third Crusade prepare to leave Europe.

Above: The Templars were warrior monks. Their group, or order, was founded around 1119 to defend Christian pilgrims travelling to Jerusalem. Later, Templars led armies of Crusaders fighting against Saladin in the Holy Land.

War Leaders

RICHARD I

Richard I 'the Lionheart' was king of England from 1189 to 1199. Richard was tall, strong, brave and intelligent. He was respected by Muslim enemies as well as his Christian comrades. Saladin's own biographer noted that Richard 'possessed judgement, experience, braveness, and cleverness... and cunning'. He added, 'Never have we [Muslims] had to face a bolder or more subtle opponent.' After failing to succeed against Saladin, Richard planned to return to the Holy Land to lead another Crusade. However, he was killed in France, while besieging a castle.

Below: This image of Richard I is taken from a French manuscript written in 1240.

PHILIP II AUGUSTUS

Philip II Augustus (1165–1223), seated on the left, was at war with Richard the Lionheart when the pope called for a Third Crusade. The two men agreed to make peace and join forces to go on Crusade. Philip became ill with dysentery soon after arriving in the Holy Land. He returned to France, where he swiftly invaded Richard's lands.

BARBAROSSA

Frederick I, nicknamed Barbarossa, 'Red-beard', was the most powerful ruler of Europe. He ruled his empire with a strong hand, introducing tough new laws to bring order to rebellious provinces. Clever, brave, energetic and a good leader, he was eager to learn and seek new experiences. He made many friends – and powerful enemies. In 1188, Barbarossa decided to join in the Third Crusade. He summoned a vast army and set out for the Holy Land. His death in 1190 – he suffered a heart attack and drowned while trying to cross a river – seriously weakened the Christian side.

The Third Crusade

The leaders of the Third Crusade assembled a fearsome fighting force. They set out from Europe with hundreds of ships and over 50,000 men. Before they reached the Middle East, however, disaster struck. In June 1190, Frederick Barbarossa, who was travelling overland through Byzantine and Seljuk Turkish territory, drowned while swimming across a river. Without their leader, many of his men decided to go home, while others were killed by Seljuks. Only a few reached the Holy Land.

Barbarossa was the most famous Christian ruler. Muslims must have hoped that the Third Crusade would fail without him. They did not know that Richard I, the new young king of England, would prove to be a brilliant soldier and commander.

Richard landed close to the city of Acre in June 1191. Like Tyre, Acre was an important harbour, but it was ruled by Muslims. A small Christian army that had attacked Acre earlier was trapped outside the walls by troops loyal to Saladin. Right away, Richard took command of all the Crusaders. He surrounded Saladin's men and ordered huge battering rams and mangonels built to smash down Acre's walls.

Mass murder?

At Acre, Richard took 2,700 Muslim prisoners. To ransom them, he demanded 200,000 gold coins and 500 Christian captives, plus a priceless Christian holy relic – the remains of the wooden cross on which Jesus died. This had been captured by Saladin at Jerusalem. When Saladin heard these demands, he refused to pay, so Richard killed his prisoners.

June 1190
The Crusader leader Emperor Frederick Barbarossa dies.

June 1191
Richard the Lionheart arrives in the Holy Land.

Just one month later, the city surrendered. After that, Richard led the Crusader army south toward Jerusalem. As before, Saladin hoped that the dry desert land would help defeat the Crusaders. But Richard had learned from what he had heard of the Crusaders' sufferings on their march to Hattin. He ordered his fleet to sail south along the coast, to supply food and water to all his men as they marched. Saladin's soldiers shot the Crusaders with bows and arrows, and deafened them with loud trumpets and drums, day and night. But Richard and his Crusaders marched on.

Christian and Muslim armies came face to face on 7 September 1191, at Arsur. At first, it seemed as if Saladin and his Muslims would win. They attacked the Crusaders boldly, and killed many of their horses. Richard called on his soldiers to stand firm, but the Christian Templar knights, in the frontline, galloped toward the Muslims. Richard realized that he must follow. He led the rest of his army in a heroic charge against Saladin's army. To everyone's surprise, Saladin's troops scattered and ran away.

Right: Crusader troops, armed with bows and arrows, fire on Muslims inside the city of Acre during the siege of 1191. The Muslims throw rocks down on their attackers.

June 1191
Richard the Lionheart captures Acre from the Muslims.

7 September 1191
Richard the Lionheart defeats Saladin at the Battle of Arsur.

Peace at Last

The Battle of Arsur was the first time Saladin had been so badly defeated. It was a great blow to his pride and prestige, but he fought on. In September 1191, Richard's Crusader army reached Muslim-held Ascalon, the most important fort between Egypt and Syria. Saladin could not risk it falling into Christian hands, so he gave orders to destroy it completely.

Richard rebuilt Ascalon, and then, in December 1191, led his army to attack Jerusalem. The Crusaders' progress was painfully slow. They ran short of food and were fired at by Saladin's 'hit-and-run' archers all the time. By January 1192, they still had not reached Jerusalem. Sorrowfully, Richard turned back. He realized that, unless he could conquer – and hold – the Muslim land around Jerusalem, he would never capture the city. The Crusaders were bitterly disappointed. They felt cheated and betrayed.

'The king was a giant in battle, and [was] everywhere in the field, now here, now there, wherever the attacks of the Turks raged most fiercely... his sword shone like lightning and many of the Turks felt its edge. Some were cloven in two from their helmet to their teeth; others lost their heads, arms, and other limbs, lopped off by a single blow.'

Description by a Christian chronicler of Richard the Lionheart fighting

Autumn 1191
Saladin destroys the coastal fort of Ascalon. Richard the Lionheart rebuilds it.

January 1192
Richard the Lionheart fails to recapture Jerusalem.

Right: Thanks to his diplomacy and skill on the battlefield, Saladin became famous throughout Europe, as shown by this portrait of him in an Italian manuscript dating from 1450.

The Crusaders had left their families and risked their lives to try to recapture Jerusalem. Was there really no hope of succeeding? Richard listened to their protests, and led them off to fight again. In June 1192, the Crusaders reached the mountains surrounding Jerusalem. From there, they could look down on the holy city, but that was as close as they ever came. They retreated again, to the coast.

All this time, Saladin had been watching and waiting. Now he seized his chance to attack. The Crusaders were tired and miserable. In August 1192, Saladin launched a fierce assault on the Crusaders, who were sheltering at Jaffa and Ascalon. Richard and his men fought back bravely – and drove the Muslims away. By now, Saladin had lost three major battles, and Richard had failed to recapture Jerusalem. Neither would admit defeat, or could claim complete victory. It was a stalemate. Exhausted, they agreed to seek peace.

June 1192
Richard the Lionheart makes another failed attempt to capture Jerusalem.

August 1192
Saladin fails to defeat the Crusaders at Jaffa and Ascalon.

New Rulers

In September 1192, Richard and Saladin signed a solemn treaty – the Peace of Ramla. In it, they agreed that Muslims should rule Jerusalem, while Christians could keep a narrow strip of land along the Holy Land coast. By now, both Richard and Saladin were ill. Richard was suffering from dysentery and Saladin was weak after years of fighting. They had lost many soldiers and were running short of money – and they had enemies to fight elsewhere. Both needed rest and both wanted peace.

Richard and his surviving Crusaders sailed away from the Holy Land on 9 October 1192. Saladin went to his favourite city, Damascus. There he hoped, at last, to do what he liked best: spend time with scholars, writers, religious teachers and friends. He looked forward to sitting with his guests in the beautiful gardens of Damascus, enjoying the cool evening air. They might eat fruit or talk, play chess and listen to readings from the Qur'an. Saladin also looked forward to leafing though his private notebook, where he had copied down extracts from his favourite books, manuscripts and poems.

Wartime wedding

One of the most famous stories about Saladin describes how his troops were surrounding a Crusader castle when he learned that a wedding was going to take place inside. He sent a messenger to ask which tower would be used for the ceremony and ordered his men not to shoot there. To show her thanks, the bride's mother sent Saladin a basket of cakes from the wedding feast.

9 October 1192
Richard the Lionheart leaves the Holy Land forever.

4 March 1193
Saladin dies in Damascus.

Sadly, Saladin did not live long enough to enjoy the peace and quiet with his friends. He grew weak and could no longer eat even the simplest food. His Jewish doctor, Maimonides – the best medical man in the Middle East – prescribed barley water and boiled rice, but these failed to cure Saladin. He died at Damascus on 4 March 1193, at the age of 54. Muslims throughout the Middle East mourned his passing with words from the Qur'an: 'Indeed, God is on the side of those who do good.'

No one could replace Saladin, as a ruler or warrior. After his death, his family argued over the division of his empire. In 1200, Saladin's brother al-Adif Sayf al-Din finally took control over Egypt. The Ayyubid dynasty, which Saladin had founded, stayed in power there until 1260.

Saladin's eldest son, al-Aziz Uthman, spent years fighting – and failing – to take over Egypt from his uncle. Saladin's second son, al-Adfal Ali, ruled Syria. Saladin's third and favourite son, al-Zahir Gazi, Prince of Aleppo, followed his father as a war leader. Al-Zahir's battle-skills were soon needed. In 1197, a fresh Crusading army arrived in the Holy Land.

Left: A medieval mosaic from the Great Mosque in Damascus shows fine buildings surrounded by peaceful countryside.

1197
The armies of the Fourth Crusade arrive in the Holy Land.

1200
Saladin's brother, al-Adif Sayf al-Din, wins control of Egypt.

After Saladin

Today, Saladin is remembered as a great war leader who conquered an empire and drove invaders out of his homeland. He is honoured as a Muslim hero, a fighter for his faith, who led a jihad to recapture the city of Jerusalem and restore Muslim worship there. He is admired for his skills at organizing a vast army, planning battles and ambushes, and inspiring loyalty among his men. He is respected for his love of learning, generous gifts to charity and personal devotion to his religious beliefs.

Above: For over 300 years after Saladin's death, Muslims and Christians continued fighting in the Holy Land. This manuscript shows the troops of King Louis IX of France, who led two more Crusades in the 13th century.

There was also something unusual – and very special – about Saladin. Looking back on his own life, Saladin said, 'I have become as great as I am because I have won the hearts of men by gentleness and kindness.' These are rare qualities for any leader, but many stories tell how Saladin helped women and children, treated enemies with mercy, and was gracious to rich and poor, whatever their faith.

But Saladin was not perfect. He spent many years winning land for himself before he decided to defend the Muslim faith.

1221

The Ayyubids – the ruling dynasty established by Saladin – defeat the Fifth Crusade in Egypt.

1260–61

The Mamluks defeat the Ayyubids and take control of Egypt and the Middle East.

He failed to defeat the Crusaders completely, or to end the Christian invasions of the Holy Land. He also failed to arrange for a peaceful hand-over of power to his sons. Unlike earlier Middle Eastern leaders, however, Saladin did succeed in uniting Muslims to fight under his leadership, and forced Richard the Lionheart, the greatest Christian warrior of his age, to retreat to Europe and never return.

The Crusades continued long after Saladin was dead and buried. Christians and Muslims went on fighting in the Middle East until the 16th century. Men on both sides were brave, and suffered terribly. Families were destroyed, and communities were divided. Worst of all, the Crusades led to bitterness and misunderstanding between people of two great civilizations, Christian Europe and the Muslim Middle East. Tragically, the memory of this ancient, epic struggle still causes conflict between some Muslims and Christians today.

Left: This modern statue of Saladin in Damascus shows him riding into battle on a war horse.

1291
Crusaders lose all their land in the Middle East. They move to Cyprus and the Greek island of Rhodes.

1453
The Ottomans capture Constantinople. This marks the end of the Christian Byzantine empire.

Glossary

arcade a covered walkway.

astronomy the scientific study of the planets, moons and stars.

Ayyubid the ruling dynasty established by Saladin.

barley water a soothing drink made by soaking grains of barley in water, then adding fruit juice, sugar or honey.

besieged surrounded on all sides and trapped by enemies.

Byzantine something that relates to the Byzantine Empire. This was an empire that covered an area of eastern Europe from the fall of the Roman Empire in the fifth century A.D. until 1453, when it was conquered by Turks.

caliph the spiritual and political leader of the Sunni Muslim community in Saladin's time. Caliph means 'successor' or 'deputy' of the Prophet Muhammad.

calligraphy the art of creating beautiful handwriting. In Saladin's time, calligraphy was used to decorate Muslim religious buildings and make copies of the Qur'an.

cavalry soldiers on horseback.

chronicler a person who writes down a record of important events.

citadel a walled area within a city.

compassionate to be full of kindness for other people.

Crusaders Christian knights and soldiers who made repeated attempts to take control of the Holy Land from Muslims.

devout to be devoted to religion.

dhow a type of sailing boat used by Muslim traders.

diplomacy helpful discussions between powerful people from different countries.

dynasty a ruling family.

fast to go without food.

Fatimid a Muslim dynasty founded in Tunisia. In the tenth century A.D., the Fatimids conquered Egypt.

Hadith sayings of the Prophet Muhammad that have been recorded and passed down by Muslim scholars.

harem private rooms for women in a Muslim house.

Holy Land the territory close to the city of Jerusalem in the Middle East. It was, and still is, holy to people from three great faiths: Christians, Muslims and Jews.

ivory the hard, white material of elephant tusks.

jihad an Arabic word meaning 'struggle for good'. Often used to mean 'holy war'.

Kurd a member of a people who live mainly in northern Iraq, eastern Turkey and western Iran. Most Kurds are Sunni Muslims.

madresseh a Muslim college.

mangonel a giant catapult that hurls rocks.

martyr a person who is willing to die for their faith.

meditation thinking deeply. Religious people from many faiths meditate to help them feel closer to God.

minaret a tall tower close to a mosque from which Muslim worshippers are called to say prayers.

monsoon Asian winds that bring heavy rain. Monsoons occur at the same times each year.

mosque Muslim place of worship.

Muhammad prophet who founded the first Muslim community, and preached the faith of Islam. He lived from A.D. 570 to 632.

multicultural relating to the cultures of many different peoples.

Muslim a follower of the religion of Islam. Muslims believe in one God, Allah, and honour the Prophet Muhammad.

Nilometer a device used to measure the rise and fall of the River Nile.

overlord a ruler who holds power over lesser rulers.

pilgrims people who make a journey, for religious reasons, to a holy place.

plunder to steal valuable items, particularly during a war.

prestige fame and respect.

prophet a messenger from God or a religious teacher.

Qur'an the Muslim holy book.

Ramadan the ninth month of the Muslim calendar, during which devout Muslims fast (take no food) between sunrise and sunset.

ransom the payment demanded for the release of prisoners.

recite to speak a passage out loud, often from memory.

reverently showing respect for a religion.

righteousness goodness.

Seljuk relating to the Seljuk people from Central Asia, also known as the Seljuk Turks. In A.D. 1055, they became an important power in the Middle East.

Shia a branch of the Muslim faith. Shia Muslims are guided by Imams (holy leaders) who are descended from Ali, the Prophet Muhammad's son-in-law.

souk a covered market in a Muslim town.

stalemate a situation in which opposing forces find that neither can win a battle.

strategic something planned with careful thought, especially in war.

strive to aim for, or try hard.

Sufis Muslim mystics who use poetry, music and meditation to come closer to God.

Sunni branch of the Muslim faith. Sunni Muslims follow the example set by the Prophet Muhammad. The majority of Muslims are Sunni.

truce a pause in fighting agreed by all sides.

unorthodox unusual, not according to custom.

Bibliography

The Crusades and the Holy Land, Tate, George, published by Thames & Hudson, London, 1996

The Crusades 1095–1197, Phillips, Jonathan, published by Longman/Pearson Education, London, 2002

The Oxford Illustrated History of the Crusades, Riley-Smith, Jonathan, published by Oxford University Press, England, 2001

Saladin in His Time, Newby, P. H., published by Phoenix, London, 2001

Warriors of God, Richard the Lionheart and Saladin in the Third Crusade, Reston Jr, James, published by Faber and Faber, London, 2001

Sources of quotes:

p.49 Beha ad-Din, *The Rare and Excellent History of Saladin,* translated by D.S. Richards, Sicolar Press, Aldershot, England, 2001, p.28

p.54 Quoted in *Richard the Lionheart,* J. Gillingham, Weidenfeld & Nicolson, London, 1989, p.215

Some web sites that will help you explore Saladin's world:

www.fordham.edu/halsall/med/salahdin.html
Biographical information on Saladin.

www.saudiaramcoworld.com/issue/197003/saladin-story.of.a.hero.htm
Biographical information on Saladin.

www.historylearningsite.co.uk/third_crusade.htm
Resources on the Third Crusade.

www.ucalgary.ca/applied_history/tutor/islam/
A history of the Islamic world up to 1600.

www.bbc.co.uk/religion/religions/islam/
Information and links on Islamic beliefs, history, customs and art.

Index

Acknowledgments

Sources: AA = The Art Archive, BAL = The Bridgeman Art Library, Scala = Scala, Florence,
SHP = © Sonia Halliday Photographs.

B = bottom, C = centre, T = top, L = left, R = right.

Front cover Detail of a portrait of Saladin from a 13th-century manuscript, Photo BAL/British Library,
London; **1** akg-images/Hedda Eid; **3** BAL/Bibliothèque Nationale, Paris; **4T** SHP/Bibliothèque Nationale,
Paris; **4B** Scala/National Museum, Damascus; **5T** SHP/Bibliothèque Nationale, Paris; **5B** Scala/British
Library, London; **7, 8, 9** SHP/Bibliothèque Nationale, Paris; **10** Getty Images/Lonely Planet Images;
11 SHP/Bibliothèque Nationale, Paris; **12** AA/Harper Collins Publishers; **14** BAL/© The Trustees
of the Chester Beatty Library, Dublin; **15** SHP/Bibliothèque Nationale, Paris; **16C** BAL/Topkapi Palace
Museum, Istanbul; **16B** Scala/Louvre, Paris; **17T** Scala/Bargello, Florence; **17B** AA//Dagli Orti;
18, 19 SHP/Bibliothèque Nationale, Paris; **21** Scala/National Museum, Damascus; **23** BAL/Bibliothèque
Nationale, Paris; **24** BAL/British Library, London; **26** BAL/British Library, London; **27** SHP/Bibliothèque
Nationale, Paris; **28** BAL/Oriental Museum, Durham University; **31** SHP/Jane Taylor; **33** SHP/Bibliothèque
Nationale, Paris; **35** BAL/British Museum, London; **36** BAL/British Library, London; **38C** SHP/Verity
Weston; **38BR** Scala/Camposanto, Pisa; **39TR** AA; **39CL** AA/Palazzo Pitti, Florence/Dagli Orti;
39BR AA/Museum of Islamic Art, Cairo/Dagli Orti; **41** BAL/Bibliothèque Nationale, Paris; **42** SHP/James
Wellard; **43** SHP/Jane Taylor; **45** Scala/British Library, London; **47** The Master and Fellows of Corpus
Christi College, Cambridge; **48** BAL/British Library, London; **49** SHP/Bibliothèque Nationale, Paris; **50TL**
AA/Templar Chapel, Cressac/Dagli Orti; **50B** BAL/British Library, London; **51T** akg-images/British Library,
London; **51BR** akg-images; **53** Scala/British Library, London; **55** BAL/British Library, London; **57** SHP/
Jane Taylor; **58** SHP/Bibliothèque Nationale, Paris; **59** akg-images/Hedda Eid.